Toxic Leaders

Are They Poisoning Your Workplace?

Gianna C. Clark

Limit of Liability / Disclaimer of Warranty. The author makes no representation or warranties with respect to the accuracy or completeness of the contents of this book and specifically disclaim any implied warranties of merchantability or fitness for a particular purpose. The advice and strategies herein may not be suitable for your situation. You should consult with a professional where appropriate. Neither the publisher nor author shall be liable for any loss of profit or any other commercial damages, including but not limited to special, incidental, consequential or other damages. People or companies portrayed in this book are illustrative examples based on the authors' experiences, but they are not intended to represent any one person or organization.

Cover Photo by Danilo Alvesd on Unsplash

Copyright © 2021   Gianna C. Clark

All rights reserved, including the right of reproduction in whole or in part in any form

Printed in the United States

Second Edition

ISBN: 978-1-387-13911-8

Acknowledgments

Seldom do we accomplish anything without the help and support of others. Thank you to my friends and colleagues who encouraged me to put pen to paper.

CONTENTS

Acknowledgements

Introduction   1

Setting the Stage

    Leadership Matters   5

    The Toxic Work Environment   7

    The Toxic Leader   11

The Case Studies

    The Good Ole Boys   15

    The Bully   27

    The Control Freak   39

Dealing with Toxic Leaders   55

Is There an Antidote?   67

About the Author   73

Introduction

Leadership.

It's the single most important variable in a company's success. Hundreds of books and articles are devoted to the topic of leadership, providing strategies for leadership development and describing attributes and competencies of great leaders.

With all this focus on leadership, one might think that toxic leadership went out with the era of robber barons and speakeasies. But toxic leaders are still with us.

In fact, they exist in many organizations. Their behaviors vary, but their impact is the same: they poison the workplace.

Toxic leaders are at the root of low employee engagement, stifled innovation and high employee turnover. Through their actions or inaction, they are the keepers of the toxic workplace.

Toxic Leaders come in many shapes and sizes. Whether you find yourself surrounded by Good Ole Boys, are being crushed by a bully, or are at the mercy of a Control Freak, the impact is the same. It's pure poison.

Sound serious? You bet it is.

In this book, we'll first set the stage by describing a toxic work environment and defining various toxic leader behaviors that contribute to this outcome.

Next, three case studies will describe how toxic leader behaviors impact individuals and the organization as a whole. Following each case study is a summary of lessons learned and a few discussion questions to help readers focus on behavioral impacts.

We wrap up by looking at the pros and cons of various alternatives for dealing with a toxic leader and exploring the antidote.

Join me as we mingle with the "Good 'Ole Boys", fight back a Bully Boss and escape the bonds of a Control Freak. Will we survive?

Read on and find out.

SETTING THE STAGE

Leadership Matters

The Toxic Work Environment

The Toxic Leader

Leadership Matters

Great leaders are the heart of great organizations.

They create a work environment that garners trust, facilitates inclusion, sparks innovation and engages employees. They do this by being fair and objective, allowing their employees a voice in the process, connecting employees to a purpose, providing professional development and career opportunities, and appreciating, recognizing and rewarding employees.

I've worked for a few leaders who have had these skills. They believed in me, gave me opportunities, and helped me to learn and grow. It was their coaching, guidance and support that enabled me to establish a successful career that over 30 years allowed me to advance from an entry-level associate position to the vice presidency of a Fortune 500 company.

These leaders challenged me to do more than I thought I could, counseled me when I went astray, held me accountable for results and, when I delivered, rewarded me with more opportunities.

To Andy, Jim and Jay: I am forever grateful for your leadership.

But for every great leader, there are dozens who don't make the cut. They are the keepers of the toxic workplace.

The Toxic Work Environment

When you hear the words "toxic workplace" what most likely comes to mind is a workplace filled with harassment, discrimination and abuse. The phrase creates a vision of bosses screaming and shaking their fist, inappropriate sexual behavior and retaliation for those who don't "play the game." These environments have been dubbed "hostile work environments," and the types of violations that occur are most appropriately addressed by labor laws.

A toxic workplace is different from a hostile work environment in that employees and leaders don't normally engage in "hostile" behavior as defined by law. Instead, the work environment is tainted with bias, company politics and distrust. Power is revered and employees are undervalued. These toxic behaviors undermine the workplace, resulting in poor employee morale, low employee engagement, high turnover and a cadre of employees who underperform.

Working in a toxic workplace is emotionally and physically draining. Employees spend a great deal of time learning to maneuver in the organization, figuring out who to trust, who has political power, whose bad side they don't want to be on and how to stay out of the line of fire when things go wrong.

The hallways and lunch room are usually buzzing with chatter about who got treated unfairly, the boss' favorite that can do no wrong, and why a select few get all the opportunities. Teamwork is almost non-existent as employees compete for their boss' attention and a chance to get ahead. Employee contributions seem to go unnoticed and recognition is almost unheard of. Working hard seldom gets you anywhere as you watch the select few who are hardly working land the best opportunities.

Power is the most cherished commodity. Wield it and you are golden.

Employees who have a great deal of time invested with a company have been slowly co-opted into believing that "things aren't so bad" or "it's the same wherever you go." Newer employees are either assimilated into the work place or leave. Those who try to introduce change are "not the right fit" and are dealt with accordingly.

It is often not until employees break free of a toxic workplace that they realize just how bad it was.

Toxic work places can be found in any industry. In most, three factors enable the poisonous behaviors to exist.

First, there is the fear factor. Employees are afraid of reporting toxic behavior on the part of their boss for fear of damaging their employment status. If employees speak up, they might get labeled as non-team player or as having trouble "getting along." Once this perception is established it can damage chances for a promotion or future opportunity. It is a practice known as "soft retaliation." The labeling is done with such finesse, it is hard to prove actual retaliation. And if an employee wanted to file a legal charge, good luck fighting the corporate lawyers.

The second factor is an outgrowth of the first. Employees learn that when toxic behavior is reported, nothing is done about it. Since most toxic behavior does not cross the line of violating labor law, chances are slim that the behavior will be addressed in a finite manner. Additionally, employees observe how those who report toxic behavior are treated and decide to keep their heads down rather than risk their own careers. As a result, the toxic behavior goes unreported and the behavior continues. Those who don't want to deal with it usually leave the company.

Where is the Human Resources (HR) department in all of this and why are they not taking action to address the behaviors? An effective HR organization can help keep toxic leaders at bay if they have the courage and power to serve-up the elixir. But as poison begins to creep into an organization, HR can be affected as well.

In many instances HR employees are either part of the toxic culture or afraid to challenge it. They are the third factor that can facilitate a toxic workplace. When, no matter the circumstance, HR consistently sides with management, soft pedals complaints or simply looks the other way, employees quickly realize that reporting issues to HR won't make a difference.

And so the toxic workplace is allowed to flourish, facilitated by toxic leaders and sanctioned by those willing to look the other way.

The Toxic Leader

Toxic leaders poison their workplace by exhibiting some or all of the toxic behaviors listed below.

Autocratic: Rules with an iron fist. Exercises power as a right. Disregards employee voice.

Biased: Decisions lack fairness and equity. Plays favorites. Non-inclusive and cliquish.

Controlling: Values power. Micromanages. Undervalues input.

Distrustful: Trusts no one. Checks behind employees. Self-validates information.

Egotistical: Arrogant. Exaggerated sense of self-importance. All about themselves.

Intimidating: Makes employees feel ignorant or inadequate. Instills fear. Oppressive.

Manipulative: Strategically controls an outcome through divisive means. Scheming. Cunning.

Political: Places office politics and self-gain above the team. Seeks favor. Plays the game.

Untrustworthy: Waffles on positions. Takes credit for others' work. Dishonest and backstabbing.

Certain combinations of these behaviors form the foundation of workplaces that foster good ole boys, bullies and control freaks. Although the story plays out differently in each organization, most toxic leaders usually have one thing in common: They are mostly concerned about themselves and their own success.

Their arrogance blinds them to their own toxic behavior – or, in the case of those who are more in tune to their toxic behavior, allows them to justify it.

It is hard to imagine how toxic leaders can exist and flourish in an organization -- that is, until you see them in action.

The case studies included in this book are illustrative examples of how toxic leaders poison their workplace.

THE CASE STUDIES

The Good Ole Boys

The Bully

The Control Freak

The Good Ole Boys

Martin had held various leadership positions in a Fortune 500 company when he finally landed a spot in the executive ranks. Martin had worked closely with a relatively new CEO, who recognized his talents and appreciated his passion for the business. Needless to say, Martin was full of excitement and anticipation.

A few days after receiving the job offer from the CEO, Martin's new boss — a senior VP I'll name Mr. Brown — offered to come to Martin's office for a meet-and-greet. Although he had met Mr. Brown on a few occasions, Martin had never worked closely with him and was looking forward to the chance to get acquainted.

It seemed like things were going well. But after the two exchanged a few social niceties, the tone of the meeting abruptly changed.

Mr. Brown leaned back in his chair, crossed his legs, tilted his head down and said, "You know, Martin, you were not my first choice for the vice president position. There are others in the company who I would have liked to see in the position. But our CEO sees something in you and asked me if putting you in this position would be a show-stopper. I told him that it wouldn't, so here we are."

The room went still. From Mr. Brown's body language, Martin surmised that his only concern at this point was making sure Martin was beholden to him for allowing him the opportunity to work for him.

After a brief pause, Martin gathered his wits and assured Mr. Brown that he was up to the challenge and would prove his worth in the coming days. Mr. Brown left after they discussed a few logistics.

Martin watched as his new boss walked across the parking lot to his car, and thought to himself "What a jerk." As time went on, Mr. Brown would prove himself worthy of this label time and time again.

Being a go-getter, Martin didn't let the "unwelcome welcome" encounter with Mr. Brown dampen his excitement, and dove right into his new assignment.

Martin spent the first couple of weeks meeting with various executives in his business area to understand their work and discuss how his team could best work with their organization. He also spent countless hours simply talking to people at all levels of the organization to get a feel for how things were run.

At first, people were a little guarded, but as employees became more comfortable with Martin, they began describing a work environment where "position" and "who you know" was the key to success.

Although Martin had heard that this particular area of the company was cliquish, he had not yet personally experienced it — until he had an introductory meeting with Mr. Vine.

Mr. Vine, who was considered the number-two man in the organization, seemed to take an interest in Martin. He asked about Martin's family, hobbies and background. The two also discussed Mr. Vine's business goals and philosophy.

Things seemed to be going well until Mr. Vine decided it was time that Martin better understood his place in the organization.

He said, "Martin, I have been in this business for a long time and have formed a strong team. I call them the 'Blue Team'. If things work out, maybe one day you can be part of the Blue Team."

Not wanting to offend Mr. Vine, Martin smiled and nodded, thanked him for his time and quickly brought the meeting to a close. As he walked out of Mr.

Vine's office, he reflected ruefully that the Good Ole Boy network that he had heard about was no rumor. It was alive and well.

Martin quickly got a taste of how things worked in the Good Ole Boy network. It wasn't long after he reported to his new position that Mr. Brown and two of Martin's peers met privately (without Martin) to discuss changes affecting Martin's department. Martin had spotted the three of them meeting in an office but didn't think much of it until the meeting broke up and Mr. Brown stopped by Martin's office to share some news.

He said "Martin, with you being new to the team, I think it would be best if we shifted the responsibility for the logistics division to one of your peers. I've already notified your director and we'll make that effective on Monday."

Stunned, Martin could only reply, "When was this decision made?"

Mr. Brown informed Martin that the decision was finalized recently but "they" had been talking about it for quite some time. Being new and not quite sure how to approach the situation, Martin replied that he would hope to be able to provide input to those types of decisions in the future and let the issue drop.

Eventually, the truth was revealed: the director who was moved out of Martin's team was unhappy that he had not been promoted into Martin's position, and did not want to report to Martin.

Since that director was one of Mr. Brown's favorites, Mr. Brown was happy to accommodate his request to be moved; after all, he had to take care of one of "the boys".

And so Martin's life with the "Good 'Ole Boys" was off to a roaring start. Over the next few months Martin tried hard to fit in; but given the culture and circumstances, he felt destined to remain an outsider.

His peers were two executives who had been with the company for more than a decade. They were the institution, the clique, the Good Ole Boys. And they made no secret of the fact that Martin was not part of their clique.

One morning as Martin was headed to the break room, he spotted his peers in the hallway having a casual chat. He thought it might be an opportunity to join in the conversation and walked up to them. Neither acknowledged him. Not a nod or a glance. Martin stood silently for about 15 seconds, which seemed like an eternity, and then slowly walked away. This type of non-inclusive behavior was rampant and served to remind those outside of the clique that being a member of the Good Ole Boys was by invitation only.

Over the next several months Martin got to witness first-hand how the clique worked its magic; those who were "in" were given special treatment, and those who weren't found themselves shuffled to the side. The Good Ole Boys were in control of promotions, raises and job assignments. Many good performers who were not part of the clique suffered the ramifications of "not belonging" and slid into mediocrity, realizing that their hard work did not pay off.

Others learned how to play the game, became pawns of the Blue Team, and were rewarded accordingly — strengthening the grip that the Good Ole Boys had on the organization.

Martin soon realized that stepping into a Good Ole Boy organization and trying to make change was almost impossible, as employees had been conditioned to "fit in". As time passed, employees on Martin's team began to appreciate his genuine leadership style and not having to deal directly with the Good Ole Boy mentality. But they were very cautious not to get on anyone's bad side, as they worried what would happen if Martin ever left the organization and they were at the mercy of the Good Ole Boys.

Martin stayed the course for several years hoping that things would change. But the depth and breadth of the crony culture could not be overcome. Although he and his team were able to accomplish some amazing things, Martin was not given opportunities or allowed to advance in the organization. It was clear that he was not and was never going to be one of the Good Ole Boys.

Eventually, Mr. Brown retired, more organizational changes ensued and a new senior leader was brought in. Unfortunately the new leader wasn't interested in breaking up the Good Ole Boy network. Instead, he hired back one of the Good Ole Boys as his right-hand man. Martin saw this as a clear sign of "business as usual" and left the organization for another position.

As for the Good Ole Boys, they promoted one of their cronies to replace Martin and were delighted to have added a new member to the "Blue Team" . . . and to their golf outings . . . and to their lunch gang . . . and to their social gatherings.

The Moral of the Story:

Blood is thicker than water and Good Ole Boys are thicker than blood.

Good Ole Boys Lessons Learned

Martin's struggle with the Good Ole Boys culture provides a glimpse of the inner workings of a leadership clique.

Good Ole Boys seek to surround themselves with people like them and they aren't shy about using their position and power to make sure people understand how things are. They are normally not abusive and don't directly insult people; instead, they foster a negative and non-inclusive work environment, as people see promotions and favoritism for clique members.

The Good Ole Boys are masterful at dealing with those who don't assimilate. This type of behavior is not only detrimental to the workplace but can lead to serious ethical problems. If someone in the clique does something inappropriate, no one is willing to risk his or her career by saying anything negative about the boss-buddy. And if an employee is asked to do something unethical by one of the Good Ole Boys, it places them in the precarious position of choosing their values over their career. That might sound like an easy choice but to someone who needs their job, it can be devastating.

The impact of a Good Ole Boy network in a workplace reaches far and wide because the behaviors that feed the culture are in every part of the organization.

Those who lead have learned how to use their relationships and power to control the organization and those who work in the organization have learned how to either play the game — or keep their heads down.

A piecemeal approach to changing the culture has little chance of success. If new leaders come in and try to work outside of the clique, they will rarely succeed; the clique finds ways to isolate them and diminish their influence as it was with Martin.

In the case of the "Good Ole Boys," most of the company -- on up through the senior leadership ranks -- knows that the business area culture is rich with the Good Ole Boy mentality. Bringing in an outsider to drive cultural change usually doesn't work as the culture is so strong that the outsider is quickly assimilated, or becomes ineffective due to isolation.

Changing one piece of the organization is not enough. True reform involves a wholesale change of behavior from the top down and throughout the leadership ranks.

Without a strong CEO willing to take on the cronyism and make broad changes in the senior leadership team, Good Ole Boys easily deal with even the toughest challenger. In most cases it's just too hard to fix, so no one does and the Good Ole Boys continue to rule.

Most CEOs will say that they cannot afford a leadership overhaul. But if they want their company to grow and improve, the reality is they can't afford to leave things as they are.

Case Study Discussion Questions:

1. Which of the following toxic leader behaviors were demonstrated by Mr. Brown? By Mr. Vine?
    - Autocratic
    - Biased
    - Controlling
    - Distrustful
    - Egotistical
    - Intimidating
    - Manipulative
    - Political
    - Untrustworthy

2. How do these behaviors impact individuals and the organization as a whole? Consider the following:
   - Severity of damage to individuals
     (Low = annoyance; High = emotional or physical stress)
   - Extent of impact
     (Low = few individuals; High = entire organization)
   - Frequency of toxic behavior
     (Low = few times a year; High = several times a week)

3. If employees are unable to leave a good ole boy environment, what can they do to minimize the negative impact of toxic behaviors on their well-being?

The Bully

Getting a new boss can cause uncertainty and anxiety, but Sally welcomed news of a change in command and chose to see it as an adventure.

Sally was a successful engineer who had made significant contributions to the organization. She never minded challenging the status quo and was always looking for a better way to serve customers.

Sally was high-energy, skilled at teaming with others and got results. People who had vision and passion described her as a "change leader." People who liked the status quo and enjoyed plodding along in the routine, on the other hand, tended to see her as a threat.

Once Mr. Rivers, Sally's new boss, got settled in his office, he asked each of his direct reports to prepare an outline to help him learn the business, and scheduled a meeting with each of them.

Sally was eager to get to know Mr. Rivers and to share her accomplishments with him. As she worked through the briefing, Mr. Rivers asked a lot of questions, but Sally was well prepared and fielded most of them with ample detail and supporting data.

Once she had completed the briefing, Mr. Rivers said, "It looks like you have accomplished a lot in the past two years." Sally glowed with pride — till the other shoe came down.

"But honestly," Mr. Rivers continued, "my primary goal is to make sure I have a strong team, and I heard that you were difficult to get along with."

Wow! Trying to stay calm, Sally asked, "Really, who did you hear that from?"

Mr. Rivers cleared his throat, leaned forward in his chair and said, "I have sources, and I like to keep them confidential."

For a moment she felt too intimidated to speak, but after a few seconds, Sally replied, "Can you provide me with some details?"

Of course Mr. Rivers insisted that any detail would divulge his sources and he was adamant about maintaining confidences. At this point, there was little left to say except that she would work hard to show him first-hand that she was a team player and could get along fine with most folks.

Mr. Rivers' answer? "Well, I hope so. I'll be watching."

Sally, who had walked into Mr. Rivers' office full of energy and excitement, now left feeling deflated and diminished. The bully had achieved his desired effect: taking Sally down a peg.

At first, Sally thought she was the only target of Mr. Rivers' bullying, but she soon realized he bullied others as well.

During a departmental update meeting, Sally observed as an employee presenting a proposal to Mr. Rivers and his staff was peppered with questions. Since Mr. Rivers was new to the organization and still learning, the questions seemed reasonable enough, and the employee answered the first round with ease and confidence.

But as the presentation went on, Mr. Rivers kept up the questions, asking for greater and greater detail until the employee could no longer answer the questions.

It soon became apparent that the line of questioning was not out of a need for information, but a need to feel superior. Having the employee get to a point where he could no longer answer questions apparently made Mr. Rivers feel powerful in some way.

Unfortunately, it made the employee feel terrible.

After noticing this interaction, Sally made of point of watching for these power plays and observed them again and again. She also noticed two discouraging effects they had on the staff.

One, people would avoid bringing up ideas or presenting for fear of public humiliation from Mr. Rivers. And two, if an employee had to present or speak to Mr. Rivers, he or she spent countless hours learning minutiae to avoid being caught without knowing some minor detail.

Working for a bully turned out to be quite a challenge for Sally and the rest of the organization. Everyone was on edge for fear of being called out, questioned, or humiliated in public.

Mr. Rivers had refined his bullying to the point that it was almost an art. Instead of name-calling, yelling or temper tantrums, he used finely crafted messages or ingeniously devised scenarios — which would always end with Sally or her fellow employees feeling bad about themselves. Some employees chose to kowtow to Mr. Rivers and avoided giving him opportunities to bully them, but Mr. Rivers constantly developed new tactics to keep employees on edge.

Sally worked hard to show Mr. Rivers that she was a dedicated employee, had good ideas and could be trusted to do her job. She worked particularly hard on a project that Mr. Rivers assigned to her related to improvements needed in a manufacturing process. Determined to prove her worth, Sally spent several days on research, industry benchmarking and team discussions to develop a potential solution.

Confident in her findings and recommendations, Sally presented her recommendations at a staff meeting — only to hear from Mr. Rivers, "I'm not sure that's the direction I want to go in. It doesn't fit how the other departments are run. You'll need to do more work on that."

Disappointed with the response, Sally got additional input from Mr. Rivers and other departments and within a few weeks presented an alternate plan. Once again Mr. Rivers indicated that he didn't think it would be a good fit because the resources needed to get it done "were going to be assigned to another project."

Again deflated, but still determined, Sally took one more whack at it and changed the project recommendations to enable work to be done using other resources.

Thinking she had all the bases covered, she again presented the recommendations to Mr. Rivers and his staff — most of whom were her peers. They too had experienced the bullying and were not willing to stick their necks out to support Sally for fear of retaliation.

With Sally's final presentation, Mr. Rivers let out a sigh, leaned across the table and said firmly, "Sally, do you know what the real problem is? You've been in here three times with three different solutions. It's like you cannot make up your mind. Let's just put this project on the back burner until you can figure out what we really need to do."

Clearly, in trying to satisfy Mr. Rivers, Sally had only ended up looking like she couldn't make a decision.

Mr. Rivers had orchestrated the perfect scenario to set Sally up, and she had fallen for it. The bully had won again.

It was apparent that there was no pleasing Mr. Rivers and that trying to make things better would only hit a dead end. The impact that this had on Sally was both physically and mentally depleting. She was under constant stress and was always having to take a defensive posture. While Sally was not the only victim, her colleagues seemed more able to let things roll off their backs.

That wasn't Sally's style, so she scheduled a meeting with Ms. Creed, the vice president of Human Resources.

As Sally described Mr. Rivers' behavior, she was overcome by emotion and found herself apologizing for her tears. Ms. Creed didn't seem surprised to hear the details, and Sally had a hunch this was not the first time someone had been to HR about Mr. Rivers.

A few weeks went by and Ms. Creed met with Mr. Rivers to discuss the situation, after which she called Sally to let her know that Mr. Rivers had been "talked to" and things should be okay.

Instead, things only got worse. Mr. Rivers came down even harder on Sally. As a result, no one else would come forward to complain about Mr. Rivers. They saw that nothing was done to stop the bullying and they were keenly aware of how Sally was being treated after she reported the bullying.

The situation quickly reached a breaking point where dealing with the daily dose of bullying and humiliation from Mr. Rivers was almost unbearable. Sally was physically and psychologically exhausted from the stress and decided to look for opportunities in other business areas.

Fortunately for Sally, her reputation as a strong performer that delivered results allowed her to quickly find a position in another part of the company. In time, and with the help of her new boss, Sally was able to quickly regain her self-confidence and courage. Her experience with a bully boss reinforced her own commitment to always be respectful of others and above all, never make anyone feel like they are not valued.

As for Mr. Rivers, HR didn't get any more complaints about him but rumor has it that employee turnover in his business area has spiked. Must be the economy.

The Moral of the Story:

If you cannot change the cards you are dealt, then take control of how you play your hand.

The Bully Lessons Learned

Although it may seem hard to imagine, the type of workplace bullying that Sally experienced is not that uncommon. And from an organizational standpoint, it can have a paralyzing effect.

People are afraid of a bully, especially one in a leadership position, and tend to go along with his or her decisions even if they aren't good for the organization.

Additionally, good ideas are not brought up, as people are afraid of being humiliated if the bully doesn't like them.

But the biggest danger of having a bully in leadership is that people won't bring up problems or issues, leaving them to fester and grow. No one wants to bring the bully bad news, since the bully is likely to shoot the messenger. And no one dares challenge the bully for fear of facing his/her wrath.

For the most part, a bully's impact on the workplace is confined to their sphere of influence. The good news is that removing a bully boss that resides at a lower level of the organization can fix most things. With the bully gone, people can begin to recover their self-worth and dignity.

The bad news is that the higher up in the organization a bully resides, the greater the impact and the greater the damage to the organization. The everyday emotional turmoil brought on by working in a bullied environment will eventually take its toll and employees will either become submissive or be constantly stressed by the bully's bashing. Either way, it will be difficult for the organization to reach its full potential.

Bullies seem to have a knack for surviving. Most people know who the bullies are and try to avoid them. If someone finds the courage to report the bullying behavior, the bully gets a "talking to" and the person who reported them usually falls victim to "soft" retaliation. Others in the workplace see this dynamic and become tolerant of the bully rather than face the same fate. Bullies rule by fear and intimidation. And with everyone afraid to challenge their behavior, they keep spreading their poison.

Removing the bully is the first step to making things right. The harder chore will be nurturing the organization back to health.

The valuable lesson that Sally learned is that being right doesn't necessarily mean that you can make things right. When dealt a bad hand, you need to know when to fold.

Case Study Discussion Questions:
1. Which of the following toxic leader behaviors were demonstrated by Mr. Rivers?
    - Autocratic
    - Biased
    - Controlling
    - Distrustful
    - Egotistical
    - Intimidating
    - Manipulative
    - Political
    - Untrustworthy

2. How do these behaviors impact individuals and the organization as a whole? Consider the following:
    - Severity of damage to individuals
      (Low = annoyance; High = emotional or physical stress)
    - Extent of impact
      (Low = few individuals; High = entire organization)
    - Frequency of toxic behavior
      (Low = few times a year; High = several times a week)

3. If employees are unable to leave a bully boss, what can they do to minimize the negative impact of toxic behaviors on their well-being?

The Control Freak

When Derrick accepted a position as director of operations support for a large manufacturing company, he was looking forward to being able to make a difference. After all, the leaders with whom he had interviewed were proud of their accomplishments and touted their organization as a top-performing team.

Derrick spent his first few weeks getting to know the leadership, his peers and his team and asking them for input related to his department. Everyone seemed friendly and accommodating, and most of his colleagues were open about improvements needed in the parts-assembly department. Derrick's background and experience enabled him to quickly hone in on needed improvements, and he was excited about the prospect of bringing positive change to the workplace. But over time, his excitement began to wane and to be replaced with uneasiness.

The first indicators of trouble appeared as Derrick familiarized himself with company policies that covered everything from time off and expenses to rewards and pay increases. The policies seemed reasonable, with different levels of management having varying degrees of autonomy to manage their teams. The problem was that for this organization, written policies were not the actual policies.

As Derrick began making personnel decisions or changes that were within his scope of authority, he was quickly advised by his human resource department that he needed to submit these types of decisions for review and approval by his group president, Mrs. Daniels.

When Derrick noted that was inconsistent with the rules described in company policies, HR replied, "In this organization, Mrs. Daniels makes 'da rules."

And so it was. Every personnel move, pay increase, or performance rating had to be approved by Mrs. Daniels, even when company policy merely required a director or manager approval. Mrs. Daniels controlled everything -- from production schedules to budgets, project scope changes, and time off. And she wasn't shy about refusing to approve something if it didn't suit her fancy.

Derrick had a personal encounter with Mrs. Daniels' controlling grip one day when he wanted to recognize one of his employees who had done an extraordinary job in increasing production run time.

Toxic Leaders

The company cash award policy allowed directors to provide monetary rewards to employees who had accomplished something exceptional. To keep standards consistent across the company, the policy for the cash awards included a checklist to determine an appropriate range for the award amount.

Derrick completed the checklist and recommended a cash award in line with the policy criteria. Being cautious, he recommended the minimum amount of the recommended range. Derrick then met with Mrs. Daniels to discuss the award and review the paperwork.

After Mrs. Daniels reviewed the information, she pursed her lips and said, "The award amount is too much." Derrick went over the scoring criteria with Mrs. Daniels and showed her that the cash award amount was the minimum recommended by the corporate policy that was used by the rest of the company and based on the scoring criteria.

Mrs. Daniels said she appreciated Derrick's input, but her decision was final. If he wanted the award approved then he would have to cut the award amount by 30 percent. Derrick was disappointed but realized that he was in a no-win situation; Mrs. Daniels' expression was one of self-satisfaction that she was calling the shots.

The Stories

Derrick thanked Mrs. Daniels and returned to his office. From Derrick's perspective, Mrs. Daniels wasn't "in control" -- she was a control freak. Unfortunately, Derrick had not spotted this during his job interview.

For Derrick, it was just the beginning of a long and painful journey that would eventually take its toll.

Derrick had been in his role a few months and was learning how to navigate the command and control environment. It was difficult to get anything done, as everything had to funnel through Mrs. Daniels, and Mrs. Daniels was always short on time. Derrick was getting less and less engaged as he realized that he wasn't going to be able to do much without the constant oversight of Mrs. Daniels.

But one day, to his surprise, Mrs. Daniels asked Derrick to take the lead on a segment of the company's business plan related to employee development. Derrick had demonstrated a keen interest in developing employees and was excited to have the opportunity.

Given six weeks to develop the framework, he immediately put things in motion. He asked for a representative from each key department to serve on his development team, and made sure his team meetings were well organized and included input from everyone.

The first team meeting was interesting in that many of the participants seemed somewhat unengaged. When Derrick probed, several team members told Derrick that they frequently worked on teams and made recommendations only to see nothing implemented.

Derrick was determined to change this practice and assured the team members that once approved, he would make sure things were put into motion. Little by little the team began to get engaged and the team members seemed to get excited about the process. As a result, some excellent ideas were presented.

Derrick invited Mrs. Daniels to address the team on several occasions and take a peek at what was going on. This was Derrick's way of getting Mrs. Daniels to buy in, a little at a time.

After six long weeks of late nights and many meetings, the team had developed a great product. Derrick was scheduled to present the recommendations to his peers and Mrs. Daniels at an offsite leadership retreat. He felt good about the product, and since each of his peers had a representative on the team, he felt confident that the recommendation would get approved.

Being new to the team, Derrick also expected that the offsite leadership retreat would be a great opportunity to get to know his peers a little better. As he watched the team interact, it became clear that Mrs. Daniels was always in control, and that Derrick's peers were all pretty much Mrs. Daniels' yes men. Over time, they had learned that as long as Mrs. Daniels got her way, their job was easier.

Just the same, Derrick thought that having had Mrs. Daniels involved in some of the project meetings might work to his advantage -- and that if Mrs. Daniels was willing to buy in, the rest of the leadership team would as well.

It was the afternoon of the second day of the retreat when Derrick finally got to present his team's recommendation. He was proud of what the team had accomplished and pleased that they were willing to trust Derrick to get things implemented.

Derrick started his presentation with a description of the process and quickly moved into the details. He wasn't even halfway through the presentation when Mrs. Daniels interrupted and said, "I just don't see how we're going to get this stuff done. It's going to take too much time and too many resources and we have more pressing things on the agenda."

Derrick tried to explain to Mrs. Daniels that the team had streamlined the process to minimize time and resource concerns, and that the benefits outweighed the time and effort three-fold. Mrs. Daniels only interrupted again and said, "I just don't see how this will work. What do the rest of you think?"

Of course, the yes men lined up and nodded their heads in agreement with Mrs. Daniels. Not one of them had the courage to disagree with Mrs. Daniels; they had been conditioned to just go along with whatever she said or face the consequences.

Mrs. Daniels then wrapped things up by saying, "Derrick, tell your team I appreciate their efforts but we'll just have to put this on the back burner for a while. Any questions?" The room was silent.

Derrick was not only stunned but disappointed. When he returned to the office, the team was eager to find out how things went. It was heartbreaking to tell them that he had been unable to get things approved. His team was disappointed, but not surprised. After all, they had seen this behavior play out often enough and had warned Derrick of what was in store. For them, it was just another iteration of busywork.

But for Derrick, it was devastating to realize that things most likely wouldn't change as long as Mrs. Daniels had such a tight grip on the organization.

From then on, Derrick continued to struggle in the organization while trying to make positive changes where he could. He reached out to his peers for help on how to deal with the controlling environment, only to find that in order to survive in the environment his peers had become control freaks themselves -- mostly to make sure that only specific information was passed on to Mrs. Daniels.

Their approach was to agree with Mrs. Daniels and avoid creating situations where they needed to get her involved in decisions. As a result, the organization experienced little change and lacked innovation.

Perhaps the most damaging attribute of Mrs. Daniels' behavior was that she didn't trust anyone. She needed to have all the details on any topic or decision so that she could develop her own conclusion and control the outcome. Mrs. Daniels' favorite saying was "trust but verify." She thought it was good practice, but it sent a clear message that she didn't trust anyone.

When people advised Mrs. Daniels of an action, she would check behind them. Sometimes she did this by asking for backup data; other times she would sneak around and get information from other colleagues. This created an atmosphere of distrust, as one employee was asked to check behind another and report back to Mrs. Daniels.

Derrick got a taste of this behavior when he brought a recommendation to Mrs. Daniels for filling one of his manager positions. Derrick had worked through the staffing process and obtained input from numerous leaders. The candidate he selected had a good track record of success and was respected by the organization.

But when Derrick approached Mrs. Daniels for approval, Mrs. Daniels said, "I think we need to get an outside perspective on your candidate. Please contact the following three consultants who have worked with your candidate on past projects, get their input and then come back and see me."

Derrick was hurt that Mrs. Daniels didn't trust Derrick's judgment on the matter. Wanting to get things done, however, he contacted the three consultants, who were all positive about the candidate. Derrick then wrote a summary report with their recommendations and provided it to Mrs. Daniels with a request for approval.

Several days passed without a response, so Derrick checked with the HR manager on the status. The HR manager responded, "It took a few days to get the approval. Mrs. Daniels telephoned each of the consultants to get their first-hand input. She wanted to make sure your assessment of their input was accurate. Seems it was and Mrs. Daniels approved the promotion yesterday."

Derrick was dumbfounded to learn that Mrs. Daniels had called each of the consultants to make sure Derrick was telling the truth.

At this point, he knew it was time to take action. Although he really enjoyed working with his department, Mrs. Daniels' "trust but verify" mentality coupled with her iron grip on every aspect made working conditions nearly impossible.

Derrick decided that he needed to discuss this behavior with Mrs. Daniels' boss in hopes that something would change.

Within a few weeks, Derrick met with the organization's CEO to discuss his concerns with Mrs. Daniels' behavior. Derrick had specific examples and translated them into how Mrs. Daniels' dictatorial ways were harming the organization. To Derrick's surprise, the CEO was fully aware of the behavior and had no issues with it. He advised Derrick to fall in line.

Derrick was disappointed with the CEOs response and thought long and hard about what to do next. Clearly, the current situation was unbearable. Management frequently encouraged employees to speak up with the promise that there would be no retaliation but Derrick was afraid that these were just empty words and could not afford to risk losing his job, at least not until he found another position. Derrick decided to keep his head down for a while hoping things would get better but also updated his resume and began searching for his next opportunity.

Mrs. Daniels was livid when she found out that Derrick had complained to the CEO. For the next few weeks, Mrs. Daniels demanded more and more of Derrick hoping to wear him down. Derrick could feel the stress but put in extra hours and weekends to make sure he delivered. He was hopeful that Mrs.

Daniels would recognize his efforts and make amends.

But Mrs. Daniels wasn't the type to make amends. She kept the pressure on Derrick until Derrick had no other choice but to leave the company. Fortunately, Derrick found a better position with a company that appreciated his leadership skills and talent.

Many employees in the organization were saddened to see Derrick leave. For a short while, he had been their only hope of change.

For Mrs. Daniels, it's still business as usual. Matter of fact, she recently commissioned a new task team to try to figure out why employee engagement scores were so low.

The Moral of the Story:

It takes great courage to keep fighting. It takes great wisdom is know when you've had enough.

Control Freak Lessons Learned

As demonstrated by Derrick's experience, control freak behaviors poison the workplace by creating a culture where decisions are driven from the top and power is considered the organization's most precious commodity.

Even if teams and groups are asked for input or are assigned a project, it's likely that the outcome will align with the control junkie's position. This type of work environment creates a huge barrier to building a successful team.

Control freaks create far-reaching and lasting damage to an organization by weakening the will and engagement of employees. Employees are hesitant to share innovative ideas that can bring needed change to the business because their ideas are mostly rejected.

Teams struggle with the environment knowing their input has little impact on the outcome, and people rarely question any decision even if they believe it might be wrong. Over time, these behaviors become ingrained in the workplace, making it difficult to repair even if the control freak is removed.

As the control freak uses his or her power to overrule policies in the workplace, it creates a cultural norm that requires "permission" for any action, further ingraining the power of the control junkie.

The most damaging aspect of a work environment that is subject to controlling behavior is a lack of trust.

Employees can't trust control freak leaders to follow policies. The control freak doesn't trust employee recommendations and works behind the scenes to constantly verify information. Employees don't trust one another because no one knows who's been tasked to check behind whom; neither do they trust that their input or opinion is valued.

Long-time employees who have learned to live with the environment are numb to it. Newer employees get a taste of the environment and usually leave.

Changing this work environment requires more than simply removing the control freak. It is likely that the controlling person has surrounded himself or herself with more control freaks, each pressing down on the organization to manage every aspect of decision-making.

A real change in the work environment will require change in several management levels and, most importantly, intervention at all levels to help employees regain trust in their leaders, confidence in their own decision-making skills and pride in their ability to make a difference.

Control Freaks are difficult to deal with because their behavior is not "inappropriate" as defined by human resource policy. As Derrick found out, they are not shy about using their power to maintain control and will go to great lengths to eliminate anyone or anything that gets in their way.

To those further up in the organization, Control Freak behavior may not be readily apparent, and if it is, many senior leaders don't think it's a problem that needs to be addressed -- so they choose not to address the behavior making Control Freaks one of the most common types of toxic leaders.

Case Study Discussion Questions:
1. Which of the following toxic leader behaviors were demonstrated by Mr. Rivers?
    - Autocratic
    - Biased
    - Controlling
    - Distrustful
    - Egotistical
    - Intimidating
    - Manipulative
    - Political
    - Untrustworthy

2. How do these behaviors impact individuals and the organization as a whole? Consider the following:
   - Severity of damage to individuals
     (Low = annoyance; High = emotional or physical stress)
   - Extent of impact
     (Low = few individuals; High = entire organization)
   - Frequency of toxic behavior
     (Low = few times a year; High = several times a week)

3. If employees are unable to leave a control freak boss, what can they do to minimize the negative impact of toxic behaviors on their well-being?

Dealing With Toxic Leaders

In each of the three case studies, Martin, Sally and Derrick were victims of a toxic leader. Although they each tried to deal with the toxic leader's behavior, the challenge was too great. For them, there was no magical ending where everything turned out fine.

This is the typical ending to most toxic leader stories. Unfortunately, in many cases, toxic leaders are allowed to remain in his or her position. If by chance a toxic leader gets removed, it would come at the expense of those who were willing to speak up.

Dealing with a toxic leader situation is no easy task. When faced with a toxic leader, you have 3 basic choices. Fright, Flight or Fight. There is not a one-size-fits-all elixir. Deciding how to address the situation involves many factors and every situation is different.

You must consider the organization itself, the culture, the leadership team and whether change is even possible. You also have to consider your personal circumstances. Can you impact change? Are you in a position to risk possible "soft retaliation" or losing your job? How will you be perceived once you challenge the toxic leader? Is the fight worth the emotional toll?

Let's take a look at the choices and weigh the positives and negatives.

Fright

Fright is usually the first and most common response. Organizations that allow toxic leaders to exist harbor a toxic environment that is chocked full of employees who live in fear. What are they afraid of?

Most are afraid that if they say something, they will be dubbed 'not a team player', 'undesirable', 'not a good fit', or whatever wugga words their organization uses to black ball an employee.

What drives this fear? Experience. Most have seen or heard of a few brave souls who spoke up and tried to make change and most likely it wasn't a happily ever after ending.

Some employees fear that they might be terminated, others fear they might not be accepted by their peers. Some fear 'not fitting in'. Whatever the fear, it keeps them from addressing the issue so instead they just keep living with it.

Living with fright can be very stressful and can impact your well-being. For whatever personal reason, if you choose to continue to work with a toxic leader, it is important to make sure it doesn't negatively impact your health, your self-confidence or your ability to be happy. So what can you do?

Don't blame yourself. You are not the cause of your leader's toxic behavior. If you have evaluated the situation and decided that your personal circumstances don't allow you to get away from the toxic leader it's not necessarily a wrong decision to stay. That being said, there are some actions you can take to minimize the personal impact.

Try to figure out your leader's mode of operation or what drives the toxic behavior and make an effort to not trigger it.

Don't let it affect your work. Toxic leaders come and go. Keep doing a good job and putting forth the effort to perform well.

You should keep a journal that details instances of your leader's toxic behavior. If things turn ugly, it's always good to keep notes to refer back to just in case. And, you never know, those journals might come in handy one day if you decide to write a book.

Keep positive. Don't let a toxic leader get to your inner self. It's easy to get beaten down when you are constantly having to put up with insults, controlling behavior or rude remarks.

When stress levels go up, take a deep breath. Refocus on something positive. Read up on articles for managing stress and apply stress-reducing techniques.

If you are not going to take action, don't talk poorly about your leader. If you have decided to stay, be professional, don't gossip and don't make things worse for yourself or others.

Last and most importantly, look after yourself. No job is more important than your well-being. Find ways to keep a positive outlook. Consider reaching out to a professional who is experienced in these types of matters and can help you deal with the daily stress of the situation. If it gets overwhelming, consider reassessing your options. Things are constantly changing and the circumstances that drove a "stay in fright" decision might change as well.

Flight

Another course of action is flight. This means you have assessed the situation and believe there is little or no chance that things will change. You might base this assessment on having knowledge that the toxic leader is a favorite of the senior leadership team or a personal friend of someone on the board of directors. Or maybe you have been made aware of previous employees who tried to address the toxic behavior but were unsuccessful.   Whatever the reason, you have assessed your individual situation and decided that it's not worth the fight and want to move on.

It's OK. You are not "copping out". Sometimes the right choice is to leave a situation that is not changeable. By all means, try to deal with the toxic behavior as best as you can while aggressively pursuing employment elsewhere.

If you are dealing with a bully, don't create situations causing confrontation. If you are working with a control freak, just buckle down and get things done. Maintain good performance so you don't get on the radar for disciplinary action. As long as you are not asked to cross an ethical or legal line, just deal with the behavior until you can exit gracefully.

In the meantime, keep a journal including detailed notes of any instances where you or one of your colleagues have felt the brunt of the toxic leader's bad behavior.

Once you obtain employment elsewhere, give appropriate notice. When the leader asks why you are leaving, it's OK to say that you were offered a better position with more flexibility, pay, benefits or whatever. At this point, creating a confrontation when you leave serves you no purpose.

If your company holds "exit interviews" you will need to decide whether you want to provide information related to the toxic leader's behavior. Most employees won't say anything negative in an exit interview as they don't want to burn bridges in case they have to use the company and/or leader as a reference at some point in time. HR might tell you otherwise but they are not the ones that have to deal with any ramifications that might arise from speaking up. Besides, HR is most likely aware of who the toxic leaders are in their organization and their failure to deal with them is an indicator that speaking up will be of no benefit to yourself or others.

Sometimes it's better to just move on.

Don't feel like you have let anyone down by not reporting the behavior. Chances are it's a known factor and there are numerous people who should be addressing the situation. Their failure to address the toxic leader's behavior is not your problem.

The pros of flight are pretty simple. Once you exit, you have rid yourself of the toxic leader and toxic work environment and can begin emotional healing.

Finding new employment may take weeks or months. In the meantime, you will need to keep dealing with the toxic behavior and not let it affect your performance or well-being. If you can, find a mentor or a professional counselor who can help you manage the daily stress caused by the situation.

If you decide to take flight, remember to keep journaling, remain in good standing, don't bad-mouth the leader, look to others for needed support and keep your decision to leave to yourself until you've landed another job.

Fight

When deciding how you want to deal with a toxic leader situation, there are several aspects of the organization that warrant consideration. Is being a toxic leader a cultural outlier or is the workplace overrun by them? If the leader's behavior is an outlier, your chances of taking action to bring about positive change is much better than if it is a deep-seated cultural issue. For example, in our case studies, Martin was faced with a network of Good Ole

Boys where just about everywhere he looked, the bias and cliquish behavior ran rampant.

A second consideration is the length of time the toxic leader has been in the organization? Are they fairly new to the organization or have they been around for ages? If the leader has been exhibiting toxic behavior for several years, it's not a secret. The fact that it has not been addressed sends a message that the behavior is tolerated. Taking them on means taking on those who have tolerated the behavior as well.

Another factor to consider is the toxic leader's overall standing in the organization. If the toxic leaders' peers all love him/her, it will be another hurdle to address. If the toxic leader is not particularly well-liked by their peers or senior management, your action may be just the thing that initiates change.

Next, you should evaluate your support network. If you fight, will others who have been victimized by the toxic leader or have witnessed the toxic behavior be willing to step forward and support your fight? Can you count on Human Resources to back you up or are they part of the problem? Fighting with a cadre of support is much different than going it alone. That doesn't mean you won't be successful, but it will most likely be more difficult.

Lastly, decide how far you are willing to go to win the fight. Once you start the process, it's difficult to turn back. Are you going to have a "conversation" with the toxic leader? Report behavior to HR? Escalate the issue to Senior Leaders? Report the issue on a company hotline? Take your fight to social media? Each of these actions has its own set of considerations and ramifications.

Since many toxic behaviors don't cross the EEOC line (meaning toxic leaders don't treat someone poorly because of their sex, age, religion, etc., they equally treat everyone poorly because they are jerks), HR may have limited power to address the issue on a legal front. Achieving a successful outcome in your fight will depend on whether upper management is willing to take action. If it's been a long-standing problem, most likely management will just 'have a little talk' with the toxic leader meaning nothing really changes. Well, almost nothing since the person reporting the issue will most likely get shunned. That doesn't mean it's not the right thing to do but you must be prepared for the do-nothing outcome and its associated backlash.

If you decide you want to fight, get your facts lined up. Refer to your detailed journal and make sure you have dates, times, who said what and any details that might be useful when reporting the toxic behavior. A good place to start the process it to seek help from Human Resources. If they are lukewarm, that will send a clear signal that you might be in shark-infested waters with no lifeboat. If HR won't help, some companies have hotlines to report things like toxic behavior but most likely the report will be given to HR to investigate. Get the picture?

I personally would love to tell everyone that they should always fight toxic behavior. But that may not be the right choice for you. Many states have laws that allow job termination for no reason. If you can't afford to lose your job, you need to think about the risk involved. No one is a better judge of your situation than yourself. If you think you can affect change with minimal backlash, go for it. If not, think about other avenues to deal with your situation.

In our case study, when Sally decided to fight it took a toll on her physical and psychological health. The entire ordeal was personally devastating and to what end?

Taking on a toxic leader is a choice. In the end, it's your choice. Just know it will be difficult, stressful and in the end, it might be better for your personal wellbeing to find a new place to work. That may not seem fair but life is not fair. Saying that is not a cop-out. It's reality.

If you choose to fight, always be respectful no matter how difficult the situation gets, don't retaliate if the toxic leader presses you and most of all take care of yourself. Life is too short. Work for someone who appreciates you.

Choose Wisely

As you can see, when faced with a toxic leader situation, there are several avenues that can be pursued. Unfortunately, none of them are easy, full-proof or without consequence. That's why it is important that you evaluate your own personal situation and chart a course that is right for you.

Whatever you choose to do, make sure you have considered all aspects of your decision and the impact it has on you personally. There will always be people egging you on to fight when they themselves won't do it. And there are always people who might tell you to suck it up and just deal with it without fully understanding the emotional pain you are experiencing. If you are having trouble sorting through it all, seek out professional help. Sometimes a counselor, therapist or coach can help you maneuver through the pros and cons in a more objective manner. They may also be able to provide suggestions on how to effectively deal with the stress.

Is There an Antidote?

At this point, some readers may be shaking their heads in disbelief -- while others can easily point to examples of such leaders in their own workplaces.

Toxic leaders such as Mr. Brown, Mr. Rivers and Mrs. Daniels from our case studies can be found in almost any company. They have been allowed to flourish because senior leaders either don't have the courage to address the situation or are not willing to expend their political capital to address a toxic leader who may be well-liked by the CEO -- else they risk their own standing. In either case, many higher-ups are content to look the other way and HR lets them get away with it.

The inability or unwillingness to address toxic leader behavior is a significant failure on the part of senior leadership.

Is there an antidote for a toxic leader? Yes, but it requires change. Because if nothing changes, nothing changes.

Even under the best of circumstances, change is difficult. In order to effect change there needs to be an awareness of the issues and desire to make a change.

Some companies may not think they harbor toxic leaders. But organizations that struggle with low employee engagement, high absenteeism and high employee turnover would be well advised to look beyond the superficial explanations for these issues and consider if toxic leaders are actually at the root of their problems. These organizations will then need to decide whether they are willing and able to make change. If so, there are basically two choices.

Either the toxic leaders change their behavior or the company changes out the toxic leader.

Changing leadership behavior is challenging, but in some instances can be successful. Coaching, mentoring and development can help leaders who are <u>willing</u> to make changes in their leadership style. This takes a great deal of time, as the leader will not only have to change his or her behavior, but reestablish his or her reputation with their peers and employees. The success rate in transforming a toxic leader is pretty low, as most have developed their leadership style over many years, and their behavior is driven by deep-rooted personality traits.

Quite frankly, I've found that deep down, most toxic leaders don't think they need to change, don't want to change and lack any impetus to do so.

Removing a toxic leader is not a one-and-done solution either. It may stop the daily dose of poison from being administered, but detoxifying the workplace will require long-term action to address the cultural damage created by the toxic leader.

In organizations led by a Control Freak, employees will need to learn how to make good decisions on their own and feel empowered to do so.

In organizations led by a Bully, employees will need to learn that they can now voice their opinion and provide input without fear of bullying or retaliation.

And organizations who experienced the Good Ole Boy network may struggle to change, since many may not want to give up the preferential treatment they enjoyed by being part of the clique.

In cases where the culture has been infused by toxic leadership behaviors, change will require that leadership behaviors be addressed at several levels. It will take a strong leader who has courage and patience to take on this task.

Making Change

If you are a leader and see similarities between how you lead and the leadership behaviors described in the case studies, you may be a toxic leader. It's time for change. Arrange for a leadership assessment, get a leadership coach and develop a plan to make change starting today. If you can't change or just don't want to, find the courage to step aside. Your organization and employees deserve better.

If you're currently working for a toxic leader, it's time for change as well. Do what you can to correct the situation but if you can't, consider finding another position. The stress caused by working for a toxic leader has long-term emotional and physical consequences. It's amazing how many people put up with toxic leaders while hoping the leader might change or get transferred. But hope is not a plan. Start planning your next career move and make the change. You are worth it, and you will be glad you did. Most people who leave a toxic leader look back and can't believe they put up with the behavior for so long.

If you are a CEO or Senior Leader and tolerate toxic leaders in your organization - shame on you.

It is the CEOs and senior leaders in an organization that have the antidote for dealing with toxic leaders. The big question is will they have the courage to serve it up?

Those who do will likely see increased productivity, improved employee engagement and reduced employee turnover.

For those who don't, let's just say they can pick their poison.

About the Author

Gianna Clark has more than 25 years of leadership experience developing strategy, building top-performing teams and achieving business excellence. Colleagues and employees describe her as having courage, makes things happen and lives her values.

A former executive at a FORTUNE 200 company, Gianna's leadership experience spans a variety of business areas including revenue management, engineering, security, regulatory affairs, supply chain, eBusiness, communications, marketing, training, leadership development and process improvement. Although very different in task and process, Gianna found that all of these areas require a common ingredient for success . . . awesome leaders.

Gianna's passion for growing and developing leaders inspired her to write the toxic leader case studies. It is her hope that the stories and lessons learned will inspire organizations to identify toxic leaders in their workplace and serve up the antidote.

Every employee deserves to work in an environment where they are respected valued and heard. It's up to leaders to make it so.

www.ingramcontent.com/pod-product-compliance
Lightning Source LLC
Chambersburg PA
CBHW070426180526
45158CB00017B/883